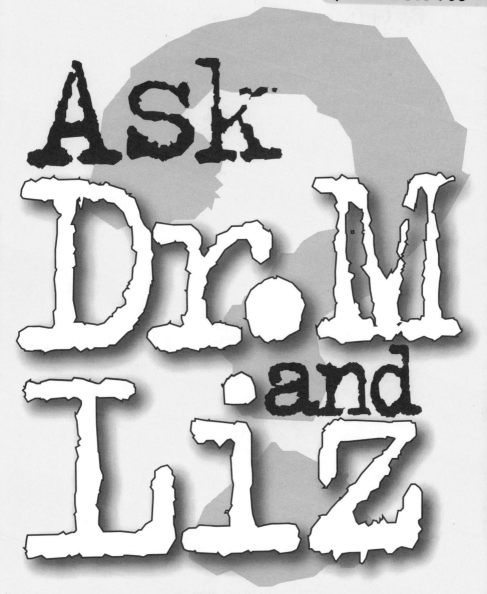

Ask Dr. M and Liz

Harriet S. Mosatche, Ph.D. • Elizabeth K. Lawner

 Girl Scouts.

Girl Scouts.
Where Girls Grow Strong℠

Publisher's Cataloging-in-Publication
(Provided by Quality Books, Inc.)

Mosatche, Harriet S., 1949-
Ask Dr. M and Liz : real answers for real girls /
Harriet S. Mosatche, Elizabeth K. Lawner

SUMMARY: Sensible advice and answers to questions submitted by real
girls from a child psychologist and her teenage daughter.

Audience: Ages 10-14.
ISBN 0-88441-692-5

1. Preteens--Life skills guides--Juvenile literature.
2. Preteens--Conduct of life--Juvenile literature.
3. Teenage girls--Life skills guides--Juvenile literature.
4. Teenage girls--Conduct of life--Juvenile literature.

[1. Life skills. 2. Conduct of life.] I. Lawner, Elizabeth K. II. Title.

HQ777.M67 2005   646.7'00835'   QBI05-700128

Harriet S. Mosatche, Ph.D.
Elizabeth K. Lawner
Authors

Cynthia B. Thompson, Chair, National Board of Directors; Kathy
Cloninger, Chief Executive Officer; Courtney Q. Shore, Senior Vice
President, Communications and Marketing; Suzanna Penn, Director,
Publishing; Edward Levy, Senior Editor; Christina Cannard-Seward,
Manager, Creative Design and Production.

Table of Contents

Table of Contents continued

Ask Dr.M and Liz about Feelings

Ask Dr.M and Liz about Your Changing Body

Ask Dr.M and Liz about Sisters and Brothers

Ask Dr.M and Liz about Parents

About Girl Scouts Your Way 137

Introduction

For seven years, my daughter Liz and I have been answering girls' questions on every topic imaginable. In this current collection, especially for tweens and teens, we look at feelings, friends, boyfriends, your body, your family—all the stuff you want to know more about. Some of the questions deal with touchy subjects it's hard to talk to others about in person. All of these issues are very real for me, having worked with girls' questions for so many years as a developmental psychologist and writer and as Senior Director of Research and Program for the Girl Scouts of the USA. We hope you find the answers you're looking for in the following pages—but keep in mind that the suggestions Liz and I make are based on our own life experiences. They may not always work for you. Consult with a parent, guardian, or other trusted adult before making important personal decisions or if you have a more serious problem.

Dr. M

My mom and I started writing our Ask Dr.M and Liz online advice column when I was nine years old. I'm 16 now and have read tons of questions and answered hundreds of them. In this book, you get advice from my mom and me, two different viewpoints to help you deal with your issues. In the journal sections, you can write down your own answers or any new questions that come to mind. Or you might just want to use that space to draw—something I love to do. If your question isn't answered in this book, you can always ask us at www.gogirlsonly.org or www.studio2b.org.

Liz

Ask Dr. M and Liz about Friends

True
Friends?

Dear Dr. M and Liz,

The other day, I was sitting with my friend at lunch and all of a sudden she said, "Do you mind if I go sit with them?" "Them" means the snobby populars. I said, "Kind of," and she left anyway. I feel bad because I felt like I got dumped for snobs. Help!

—Diva, 11

Dear Diva,

If you had been dumped for kids who aren't the "snobby populars," would you feel any better about the situation? Probably not. Being treated in an inconsiderate way by someone you care about always hurts. Tell your friend what it felt like to be abandoned at the lunch table. Maybe she'll think twice before she does it again. *Dr. M*

Dear Diva,

If your friend keeps treating you like that, I don't think she's the type you want to be friends with anyway. It's time to make some new friends who appreciate you. *Liz*

Dear Dr. M and Liz,

My friend hangs out with this girl who is REALLY mean. She calls everyone names, yells in their faces, and starts catfights with everyone. She has totally influenced my friend to believe that I was stealing from her and was searching her gym bag. Because of this other girl, my friend and I have slowly grown apart, and finally we hate each other now. She does stuff like not dressing for gym, talking trash about other people and so many other things I can't even name them all. My friend says that this other girl is a real friend, unlike someone else she knows. My other friends are being influenced by my friend and no one believes anything I say or do!

—Gooby, 11

Dear Gooby,

It's always sad to see a friendship end. But your friend has stopped treating you with any kind of respect or trust, and it's impossible to maintain a friendship without those ingredients. You can try to tell some of your other friends that what they've heard about you is not true. But if they believe your ex-friend instead of you, it may be best for you to start looking for new girls to hang out with. Don't expect to find new friends overnight—it takes a while to build true friendships. But if you continue to be the decent, caring person you are, some people will recognize those qualities and appreciate you for who you are.

Dr. M

Dear Gooby,

The first thing you should do is talk to your friend openly and honestly. If you've already talked to her and she hasn't listened, try again. Tell her how she's changed and try to get her to believe that you didn't do any of the things that you were accused of. If she still won't listen, I think it's time for you to find new friends. Anyone who thinks you're lying and is mean to you isn't worth your time and energy. I know it might be hard to try to find new friends, especially if you're shy, but if you keep on coming back to your old friend and begging her to be your friend again, she'll see it as more of a reason to treat you like dirt because you keep taking it from her. If you become friends with new people and start to have fun again, your friend might see how much of a jerk she was and want to become friends with you again. Then it's up to you. *Liz*

Dear Dr. M and Liz,

A few months ago, I had some really great (or so I thought) friends. Recently, one of them met a popular girl and decided to dump me because the other girl hated me. They've turned everyone against me. A lot of people still talk to me but only for a minute and only until someone better comes along. I know how to make friends, and I'm always friendly in my approach, but it doesn't do any good. Sometimes I feel so depressed and cry when I get home from school. I have so many secrets I want to share and so many fun times I want to have

with one true friend. I don't know what to do! Please answer this because it gets worse every day.

—Cat, 13

Dear Cat,

Your letter made it obvious to me that you are a friend worth having. It's too bad that the other girls do not recognize your wonderful qualities. At your age, friends often grow apart as interests and needs change. And popularity is seen by many teens as more important than anything else. You might try sharing your feelings (as you expressed them to me) with those friends you really want to get close to again. Perhaps they don't know how deeply their actions have hurt you. If their behavior doesn't change, use the friendship-making skills you know you have to start a new friendship. I know that there are lots of other girls who would appreciate a true friend like you to talk to and have fun with. Be open to finding one or more of them, and reach out to a trusted adult who can help you cope with your feelings of sadness.

Dr. M

Dear Cat,

If you can, try to ignore what the girls are doing to you and how they have turned against you. Continue to be friendly and caring toward your friends. After a while, they might realize how great you are and try to be with you again. But if they can't appreciate you, try to get close to a new group of people who can treat you as a true friend. Good Luck!

Liz

Dear Dr. M and Liz,

My best friend is getting on my nerves. She doesn't seem to leave me alone. How can I get some private time or tell her I don't want to be friends anymore?

—Betty, 9

Dear Betty,

Friendships—even very close ones—do not always follow a smooth course. You are dealing with one of those times when a friendship feels more like a burden than a joy. Think about whether this friendship is worth saving. If the real issue is your desire for some time away from your friend (you noted that you need some private time), let her know that even best friends need some time apart. Each of you should have time to explore individual interests. Assure your friend that time away doesn't diminish the bond of friendship. However, if you really want the friendship to end because the two of you have grown in different directions and your friendship just doesn't work anymore, tell your friend in as direct and honest a way as possible. You might say something like: "I don't think our friendship is working for us any longer. You're much more interested in . . . and I'm very involved in . . . " Emphasize that it's the relationship between the two of you that's not working so she won't think that her personal qualities are at fault.

Dr. M

Dear Betty,

Since this is your best friend, you might want to think a little bit more about whether you really do want to end your friendship. You should be honest with your friend and tell her that you need some more time alone or with other friends. If she thinks you two can still be friends, but not spend as much time together, you should try that. But if she also thinks it's best to end your friendship, then at least it ended on friendly terms.

Liz

Touchy Subjects

Dear Dr. M and Liz,

I have a best friend and we have been best friends since we were ten months old. Our moms have been best friends since they were little girls. They used to have coffee together almost every night and then they had

this big fight and haven't talked to each other for a couple of months. I rarely get to see my best friend anymore and the times we do see each other, it isn't for very long. I really miss her! What should I do?

—Help Please, 11

Dear Help Please,

It's unfortunate that you and your best friend are caught in the middle of a fight between your mom and hers. You have no control over their relationship. But you can make sure that you continue to communicate with your best friend—hard as that may be. In between the times you see each other, write letters and send e-mail messages. Be sure to let your mom know how important your friend is to you and how much you miss her. Ask your mom if she can help you find a way to get together with your friend more often. Maybe the two moms will make up, but that's their decision, not yours.

Dr. M

Dear Help Please,

Try to explain to your mom that your friendship has nothing to do with her friendship. Maybe you became friends because of your moms, but just because they're having a fight and not talking to each other doesn't mean that you and your friend shouldn't be able to see each other.

Liz

Dear Liz and Dr. M,

My friend doesn't live with her dad because he's an alcoholic. I don't like to talk about my dad around her or mention her family because I'm afraid it will make her feel bad. How do I talk to her about these touchy subjects?

— Worried About Talking, 11

Dear Worried,

You are clearly a caring and sensitive individual, which makes you a terrific friend. She knows that you are aware that her father is an alcoholic — maybe she'd welcome an opportunity to talk to you about her feelings. By bringing up something about your family, you might help her to talk about what's going on in her life. I'm sure she already knows that you would listen with compassion. If you stop yourself from talking about your family, you're creating an awkward and unnatural situation, both for you and for her. And that wouldn't be healthy for your friendship. That doesn't mean you should go on and on about how wonderful your family is (I know you wouldn't do that). And if you notice that your friend is upset by something you've shared, the two of you can talk about it. Having someone to share the good, the bad, the sad, and the funny is what makes friendship so important in our lives.

Dr. M

Dear Worried,

Find a time when the two of you are alone, and gently and simply tell her that if she ever needs to talk to you about anything that's bothering her, she can. Ask her whether there are particular topics you should avoid. Maybe she wouldn't mind hearing about your dad, but would get upset if you talked about an activity she used to share with her father — whether it's soccer or camping. By having this conversation, you'll find out what specific subjects you should avoid and your friend will know how much you care about her.

Liz

Dear Dr. M and Liz,

One day I spent the night at a friend's house and told her I was starting a band. I think she misunderstood, and she thinks that I told her she could be in it, and I already picked out the members. I don't want to hurt her feelings, but I already have too many people as it is. How can I let her down without risking our friendship?

—Stressed Singer, 13

Dear Stressed Singer,

Perhaps your friend misunderstood because she wanted so much to be in your band. Clear up this misunderstanding as soon as possible. Your friend would be very embarrassed if you discussed this with her after she had already told — maybe even bragged — to other kids about being a member of your band. Since you can't add any new members to the band itself, what about asking your friend to do promotional work—perhaps making up flyers—or organize practice schedules. The idea is to allow her to be part of the band without having her play in it. And if she has the talent you need, you might tell her she could be a substitute if someone couldn't play, or she could replace a member if someone decided to leave the band. But only do this if you would really want her in the band. Don't make a promise that you don't intend to keep, just to prevent hard feelings now. Whatever you say, be sure to remind her that you value her friendship.

Dr. M

Dear Stressed Singer,

Telling your friend you're starting a band was the right thing to do—she's your friend and you want her to know what's going on. But maybe you said it in the wrong way even though you did not mean to. You could try to talk to your friend honestly. Let her know that the members are already in it, which means that you can't let any new members in. Try to explain that the two of you had different ideas about the conversation, and that you're sorry about the misunderstanding. At the same time, do something with your friend—maybe start a club or another new activity—so she won't feel left out of your life.

Liz

Dear Dr. M and Liz,

I am adopted and I hate it when people ask private questions like "Who are your birth parents?"

–Sarah, 7

Dear Sarah,

Most of the time, people ask those kinds of questions because they're just curious, not because they want to hurt you. They probably don't realize that questions about your birth mother are very personal. Educate them — tell them how you feel and that the answer is one you'd like to keep private.

Dr. M

Dear Sarah,

The people who ask those questions probably don't know much about adoption and are just curious. But you don't have to ever answer questions that make you feel uncomfortable.

Liz

Peer Pressure

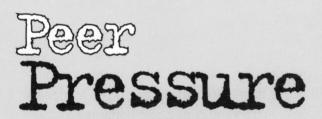

Dear Dr. M and Liz,

My friends aren't bad or anything, but at a party they tried smoking a light kind of cigarette. They asked me to try and I said no. They have never smoked before. I think they just wanted to see what it was like. Should I be friends with them?

—Lisa, 15

Dear Lisa,

First, congratulate yourself for saying "no" to peer pressure. That's great! Second, remember that friends sometimes do things that disappoint us or make us uncomfortable. As a good friend, you can try to help them avoid smoking in the future so they won't end up with a habit that will be very tough to kick. One mistake shouldn't end a friendship, but if your friends start acting in ways that continue to go against what you know is right, you might have to find new friends who share your values.

Dr. M

Dear Lisa,

If your friends don't smoke anymore, being friends with them is not a problem. If they continue to smoke, then you should help them to stop. The sooner they try to stop, the easier it will be for them. No matter what, be their friend—unless, of course, there's something else bothering you about them.

Liz

Dear Dr. M and Liz,

When I was 11, I smoked a few times and got caught. Now I'm 12 and a friend of mine smokes. She asked me to start again. I know the obvious answer is no,

but it's really addictive and I don't know what I should do—do you?

—No Name, 12

Dear No Name,

I know exactly what you should do, and so do you. Don't start smoking again. Getting caught would be the least of your problems. Smoking has absolutely no upside. If you were to start smoking again, your addiction would be even more powerful, so why would you do it? You know all about the downside—the smelly breath and hair and clothes now, the yellowing teeth, wrinkled skin, and lung, heart, and other health problems as you get older. Do yourself a big favor—don't ever put another cigarette into your mouth. And do your friend a big favor—try to convince her that she should try to stop now before it gets even harder.

D. M

Dear No Name,

The obvious answer is no, as you said—you shouldn't start smoking again. Tell your friend that you don't want to become addicted to tobacco, and if she can't accept your refusal, she's not a real friend.

Liz

Dear Dr. M and Liz,

I like reading, but my classmates don't. Some even call me a reading nerd. What should I do?

—Eli, 9 1/2

Dear Eli,

Keep reading and you'll go far. Reading is not only an important skill that you will use throughout your life, but it's fun, too! Try to ignore the name-calling, although I know it's not easy. Help your classmates to see how valuable reading is—whether they're interested in sports (they can find out about athletes), games (they'll need to read the directions), or music (they may want to study the words to a song). My love of reading helped me become Dr. M.

Dr. M

Dear Eli,

Keep on reading. It doesn't matter what the other kids say. You're your own person, so do what you think is right. By the way, a lot of kids love to read just like you do. I'm one of them!

Liz

Lonely and Left out

Dear Dr. M and Liz,

School just started, and not a single friend is in my class. How am I going to get through this year?

—A Lonely Fourth Grader

Dear Lonely,

It's hard to think about spending all day in school without your friends. But the school year just started. Look around the class—there are probably other kids who are wondering how they're going to survive without their friends from last year. Ask one of them a question, such as "What have you heard about this teacher?" to get a conversation going. One of those conversations is sure to turn into a friendship. And remember, you don't have to give up your old friends. It will just take a little extra effort to see them. But there's always lunch, recess, after school, and weekends. Dr. M

Dear Lonely,

Who says you have to give up your friends? Find ways to still see them. And spend a little time just watching the kids in your class. Then hang around one or two who seem like the type you'd like to become friends with. It'll happen!

Liz

Dear Dr. M and Liz,

My best friend and I are being separated. She's going to a different school than me. We were always together and now we're getting separated. I don't know how to live without her. Can you help me?

—Regina, 11

Dear Regina,

Although it will be harder on the two of you to stay best friends when you don't see each other all the time, if you really want your friendship to remain strong, you're both going to have to make an extra effort to stay connected. How? By calling or e-mailing each other on a regular basis and by making and keeping plans to get together after school and on the weekends. When you have a really strong bond with a friend, you'll find that when you do see each other, you'll just naturally take up where you left off—and you'll still be able to share the important things in life.

Dr. M

Dear Regina,

Last year, my best friend started going to a different school from the one I was going to. I already had one other good friend at my school, and the two of us became better friends. My best friend and I are still best friends, but now I have two best friends. I think that you should try to make new friends at your school, but also stay friends with your best friend.

Liz

Dear Dr. M and Liz,

One of my best friends is blowing me off for her boyfriend. I don't want to hurt her, but I am feeling left out.

—Left Out, 14

Dear Left Out,

Lots of girls (as well as boys) neglect their friends when they start going out with someone. Most of the time they're so excited about the new person in their lives they forget that old friendships need to be cared for. And you may be feeling just a bit jealous of the attention and time that her boyfriend is getting. If you let your friend know how you feel in an assertive but understanding way, she'll probably appreciate being reminded of how important you are in her life.

Dr. M

Dear Left Out,

Although it may seem to you like your friend is blowing you off, she probably isn't intentionally ignoring you; she's just busy with her new relationship. If you talk to her and tell her that you're feeling left out and wish you could hang out with her more, I'm sure she'll try to make some more time for you in her busy schedule.

Liz

Losing a Friend

Dear Dr. M and Liz,

My best friend just died. She meant a lot to me. Gina died the day before my birthday party, and since then I have been down in the dumps. We did everything together, even our homework. Since Gina died, my grades have really dropped. I don't even feel like doing anything.

—Mee-Mee, 13

Dear Mee-Mee,

Death is always very sad, but it's particularly difficult to accept when it happens to someone so young. And the fact that Gina was your close friend makes the situation even tougher to handle. Give yourself some time to grieve, to feel sad. That's absolutely normal. Talking to someone about Gina and your feelings might help. Perhaps you can approach a parent, or a guidance counselor at school. You'll never forget Gina, but in time, you'll find that you're able to start having fun again and to concentrate on your studies.

Dr. M

Dear Mee-Mee,

I'm really sorry about your friend dying. You probably are having trouble doing those things (like your homework) that remind you of Gina. Last summer a boy in my class died. I was really sad even though I didn't know him that well. Now, my class is raising money to start different projects that will keep his memory alive. We're going to have a special video center and a scholarship in his name. Maybe you can start something that would be related to Gina's interests. Ask your teacher or the principal in your school to help with this project.

Liz

What do you think?

_____

_____

_____

_____

_____

_____

_____

_____

_____

_____

_____

_____

_____

_____

_____

Ask Dr. M and Liz about School

School Blues

Dear Dr. M and Liz,

I don't like middle school. Every day when I arrive, I can't wait to get home. I like only one of my teachers. I'm not with any of my friends, and although I'm making more friends, I don't look forward to anything but the bus ride home. What can I do to help the day to go more smoothly?

—Alyson, 11

Dear Alyson,

Many kids have difficulty when they first begin middle school because it's so different from elementary school. It takes a while to make new friends, and to get used to the new routine of changing classes and being with different students in each subject. And you did say that you were beginning to make new friends. Give yourself some time. If you continue to find school unpleasant, talk to your guidance counselor or the one teacher you like. One of them will probably have some helpful suggestions.

Dr. M

Dear Alyson,

A lot of things go wrong when you first start middle school. During my first week in middle school, I couldn't find the school bathroom and I missed my stop on the school bus home and had to be escorted home by a school security guard. As the year went on, I made new friends. When I was really bored in class, I did my homework, or drew in my notebook. Try to look ahead to what it will be like when you've gained a little more experience in school.

Liz

Dear Dr. M and Liz,

My friend Katelyn has a problem. She does not want to go to school. When she goes, she gets all shaky and feels so sick that she has to go to the nurse. She doesn't really talk no matter how hard we try. She basically sits in guidance all day. She waits for her mom to get her. While she is there, she does the work we are doing in class. I am so worried about her. I am starting to fall behind in my work because I'm stressed about her. My parents don't really help. I need to know what to do. Please help me.

—Falling Behind, 11

Dear Falling Behind,

Your friend has a serious problem, and she needs to get help for it. Although she's fortunate to have you as her caring friend, you've gotten too wrapped up in her life. Look at how the stress of worrying about Katelyn is hurting you. Do you think that you have to be miserable because she is? The best thing you can do for Katelyn is to encourage her to get help, and to focus on getting your own life back on track. Being stressed out and falling behind in school are not going to make Katelyn's life any easier.

Dr. M

Dear Falling Behind,

You obviously care a lot about your friend Katelyn and want to help her. That's a good thing! It might be hard for her to talk to you though. Maybe you could talk to her parents or yours about getting some professional help for her, someone she could talk to. Once you know that she is getting the help she needs, maybe you will stop worrying so much about her and begin to catch up in school.

Liz

Dear Dr. M and Liz,

I'm really quiet in school. I don't socialize much with classmates. Any time I'm around other people, I feel nervous; my heart beats faster. I think something is wrong, maybe I smell or something like that. I hate this kind of life.

—Anonymous, 13

Dear Anonymous,

There's nothing wrong with you—some people just have an easier time than others socializing. Once people get to know you, they'll probably appreciate your sensitivity and other positive qualities. You're going to have to work at giving people a chance to get to know you. And the more you practice, the easier it will get. Don't expect too much from yourself at the beginning. Start with one action—maybe just smiling when you see a kid from one of your classes. (Ignore the beating of your heart; as you smile more often and to more people, your heart will settle down.) Then go on to something a bit more difficult—perhaps saying "hi" or asking a short question. When you ignore others, they might get the wrong idea and think YOU don't want to be friends with them. Take one small step tomorrow, and you'll find that the step after that will be just a little bit easier. Don't rush it—you have a whole life of socializing in front of you.

Dr. M

Dear Anonymous,

Although it may be hard, you can become more confident around people by taking baby steps. Raise your hand in class when you're absolutely sure you know the answer, and say "hello" to a classmate who seems friendly. Eventually, you'll see that there's nothing wrong with you. You just need to relax more and be yourself.

Liz

Dear Dr. M and Liz,

I'm worried about what sixth grade will be like. I'm in fifth grade right now and will be going to a new school. Could you tell me what to do?

—Worried, 11

Dear Worried,

Starting middle school can be scary, but it can also be a great opportunity to make new friends, to become more independent, to join interesting clubs. Find out as much as you can about your new school. Are there special classes you can take that weren't available to you in elementary school? Are there sports you'd like to try? Looking forward to an activity might help you feel more excited than scared. Visit the new school if you can. Becoming more familiar with a new environment is one way to take away some of the fear. Just finding out where the bathrooms, the lockers, and the auditorium are will help you feel more comfortable. Also talk to kids who are a year older than you and find out how they've managed to make it through the first year of middle school.

Dr. M

Dear Worried,

Years ago, when I switched schools mid-year, I found these tips helpful: Talk to other kids who have been in your new school and can fill you in on important details about it. Talk to your parents—they might have some helpful tips of their own.

Liz

Pain in the Class

Dear Dr. M and Liz,

My teacher is a bully! He is so mean. He does nothing but yell at us and give homework slips and detentions. What can I do?

—Anonymous, 15

Dear Anonymous,

It sounds like your teacher is using his power in an abusive way, rather than using his position to inspire and motivate you and your classmates. Unfortunately, everyone, at some time in their lives, will come across some adults as well as kids who act like that. I remember having a couple of teachers like that at your age. Often bullies need to make others feel small to feel okay about themselves. Sometimes, they enjoy using their power to hurt and humiliate. You and your classmates could ask for a meeting with your teacher. Doing this with others will probably be less intimidating than acting alone. But, if you're afraid that your teacher will become even more difficult to deal with if he's approached directly, talk to your school principal or guidance counselor. If you describe the behavior that you're observing (for instance, he often yells when a student gives the wrong answer), rather than just how you feel about your teacher (for example, he's a terrible teacher and we hate him), you'll probably get a better reception from school officials. You might also ask your parents to get involved.

Dr. M

Dear Anonymous,

Just like with any other bully, the best way to deal with your teacher is to avoid ticking him off and not letting him know that his yelling upsets you. If you and your classmates try to obey his rules, no matter how stupid they may seem, you won't give him any reason to yell at you. This however, is really only a temporary solution to your problem. The only way to really get your teacher to change his behavior is for a group of students to talk to your guidance counselor or another administrator at your school about your teacher.

Liz

Dear Dr. M and Liz,

**I have a teacher who is a pain in class. She yells
and gets mad for no reason. She's always saying "Shut
Up" and she's getting on my nerves. She was like this
even on the first day of school.**

—Frustrated, 12

Dear Frustrated,

Your teacher needs to go back to school to learn that students pay more attention and learn more when they respect a teacher and see her as a role model. Get together with the other students in your class to talk about the situation and decide what action you might want to take as a group. Start by asking for a meeting with your teacher, where you can let her know that her anger is making learning and concentrating more difficult. Also, a meeting will give your teacher an opportunity to explain why she yells so much. Together, the students and your teacher may be able to work out a better classroom atmosphere. If the prospect of talking directly to your teacher is too scary or if she just won't listen, you might ask someone else at school for advice or help—perhaps a guidance counselor or the principal. If the situation doesn't improve, ask your parents to speak to the teacher or a school official. School should be a place for learning, not yelling.

Dr. M

Dear Frustrated,

Try to focus on your schoolwork and what you're learning instead of thinking about the yelling. If it gets really bad, tell your parents. Maybe, they can talk to your teacher or your principal. I would hate it if I had a teacher who got mad all the time.

Liz

Dear Dr. M and Liz,

I am in a wheelchair and one of the class jobs is to be my pusher. I really hate it. I try to tell people I hate it and I can wheel myself and I do not need that help. It drives me crazy. I tried to speak with my teacher, but she said what she was doing was for the best.
—No More Help, 10

Dear No More Help,

From your letter I can tell that you are both competent and confident. You've already taken two actions that I would have advised—telling other students you can wheel yourself and talking to your teacher. Since neither your teacher nor the other students are listening, you'll have to get someone else to help you—perhaps a parent. It's unfortunate that sometimes adults pay more attention to another adult than to a child, even though in your case, you obviously know what is best for you. I hope your parent can convince the teacher, or the principal, if necessary, to allow you to reclaim your independence.

Dr. M

Dear No More Help,

Talk to your teacher again, but this time show her that you can wheel yourself around just fine by yourself. Also, let her know how you feel when other students have to push you around. But if your teacher is still not convinced, ask one of your parents to write a note to your teacher or meet with her.

Liz

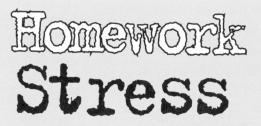

Homework
Stress

Dear Dr. M and Liz,

My teacher is really stressing me out lately with all of the work. I'm talking three to four projects a week. And about six pages of homework every night. Do you have any stress breakers for me?

—Jill, 12

Dear Jill,

Talk to some of the other students in your class to find out if they're feeling as overwhelmed as you are. If they are, you might ask some of them to join you in approaching your teacher about the excessive amount of work you've been getting and how stressed you all are. However, if you're feeling more pressured than most of your classmates, try to figure out why you're having so much trouble handling the workload. Are you having a hard time organizing your time? Is it difficult to concentrate on your work? Are you so stressed that you spend more time worrying than working? Is it hard to understand one particular subject, or are you having trouble with all of them? Discuss these questions with your teacher, a guidance counselor, an older sister or brother, your mom or dad, or another close relative. With their help, try to get at the root of your stress, and then work with them to figure out some solutions that will work for you. For example, if you're not starting your homework until after dinner, you may be too tired to work effectively. And by starting late, you may not be giving yourself enough time to get all of your work done.

D. M

Dear Jill,

Show your parents your assignment book so they'll realize how much work you have. Then you could ask your mom or dad to tell your teacher that it's very stressful to have so much homework and so many projects. Everyone needs time to enjoy themselves. You can always try to enjoy your weekends. And if you have a free day, spend some time getting a little ahead in your work so that for the rest of that week you won't be as stressed out. To reduce your stress you could play a board game or read or play with a pet or take a bath.

Liz

Dear Dr. M and Liz,

I'm doing good in school and I'm getting good grades, but I'm not doing my homework fast enough. I'm usually up until 11:00 and my mom is getting super mad at me! What should I do?

—Kathy, 11

Dear Kathy,

You didn't say when you start your homework, but that could be part of your problem. Do you have lots of after-school activities? Do you wait to start your homework until after dinner? You could also look at how you do your homework. Do you watch TV while you're working? Are you working in a place where you're constantly interrupted or distracted? Figure out what you can change to become more efficient. Look at the questions above as a guide to developing a better workspace or schedule. Since your mom is angry that you're up so late, ask her for ideas, too. Maybe she'll have some suggestions you can try. And if the real problem is too much homework, you and your mom can talk to your teachers.

Dr. M

Dear Kathy,

It's hard for me to answer since I don't know why you stay up so late. Is it that your teachers give you a ton of homework or is it that you work slowly? If you procrastinate about doing your work—even if you don't want to admit it—you should really try to stop putting off your work, no matter how hard that is for you. If your teachers give you a lot of homework, you could try to explain that to your mom, showing her that it's not your fault. If you don't whine and complain, your mom shouldn't be mad at you. If the problem is that you work slowly, try to find other times when you can start on your homework, like when you're done eating lunch or waiting for an after-school activity.

Liz

Bullies

Dear Dr. M and Liz,

At school, there is a kid (I won't say the name) who pushes me around all the time. She even slaps me. What should I do?

—Tired of Being Pushed Around, 10

Dear Tired of Being Pushed Around,

The girl who's pushing you around sounds like a bully. Does she pick on other kids too? She has no right to bully you or anyone else. You deserve to feel safe and protected in school.

Try to talk to her, but be sure to do it in a confident way. Bullies are more likely to bother kids who are shy or seem anxious. Even if you're scared inside, try not to show it. Let her know you won't tolerate being pushed around any longer. Talk to your friends about what's happening at school. A bully is less likely to bother you if she knows you have friends who will stick up for you. Involve an adult—your teacher or the school principal—if you need to. You're in school to learn, not to feel threatened or to get hurt.

Dr. M

Dear Tired of Being Pushed Around,

Tell an adult you trust about the situation you're in. Make sure she's someone who is likely to do something with what you've told her. You want the adult to do more than just listen to you. Since you're being pushed around at school, you might talk to your teacher, or you could talk to one of your parents. I hope you're able to get the girl who's bothering you to stop.

Liz

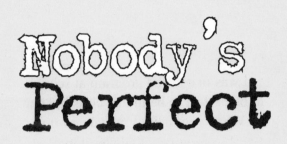

Nobody's Perfect

Dear Dr. M and Liz,

I am in the gifted program at school, and a lot of kids think I have to be perfect. I'm not perfect and they just don't understand that. Is there a way I can convince them I am not perfect?

—Mel, 10

Dear Mel,

Just continue to act like the normal kid you are. Be open to participating in activities, like sports or after-school clubs, with kids who are not in the gifted program with you. If you hear a kid talking about a music group you also like, or if you have both seen the same TV show, get a conversation started about those topics. After a while, others will realize that you are more similar to them than different from them. Help others recognize that there are many ways to be gifted, from being a caring and dynamic leader to being a great athlete.

Dr. M

Dear Mel,

When I was your age, I was in a gifted program at school, too. And if you had to be perfect to be in this class, no one would have been in it! When you make a mistake or do something that is not perfect, don't try to cover it up. Let others see that everyone makes mistakes, and no one gets 100 on every test.

Liz

Over the Line

Dear Dr. M and Liz,

There is this boy in my grade who is obsessed with girls. He says really inappropriate comments to my friends and me. Today when I was walking out to carpool, he laid his head against my shoulder and made this kissing sound. I kicked him and ran away as fast as I could. He does stuff like this to girls every day. I'm starting to get scared. We've tried to tell the teachers, but they won't take us seriously. Please answer my question! I'm not only speaking for myself, but for all the girls in my grade!

—Liz, 11

Dear Liz,

It sounds like this boy is sexually harassing you and the other girls in your grade. But using physical violence against this boy is not the answer, and besides, it probably won't stop him anyway. You were right to talk to your teachers about what has been happening to you. It's unfortunate that your teachers didn't take what you had to say seriously. Since they didn't listen, I would suggest that you take your complaint to your parents and to school administrators. You and your classmates have a right to attend school without worrying about being harassed. Keep detailed written records of his inappropriate actions, and ask the other girls to do the same—they will help you make your case. You might also want to print up your letter and my answer, and share them with your school principal. Calling this boy's behavior sexual harassment might help people understand that action must be taken.

Dr. M

Dear Liz,

It's good that you and the other girls in your grade tried to talk to teachers about your problem. I honestly don't know why they won't take you seriously, but maybe if you get your parents involved, they will. What that boy is doing is called sexual harassment, and not only is it inappropriate, like you said, but it may also be illegal. You should talk to your parents and have your friends talk to their parents, too. If you get a group of girls and their parents together to talk to the teachers or even the principal, I'm sure the school will do something to take care of the problem.

Liz

Grounded

Dear Dr. M and Liz,

You see, I skipped class to go hang out with some friends. Then my mom found out and threatened to come to school with me and walk me to all my classes. At this point, since it's the weekend, we're not talking to one another. I am in my room with the door locked and she is taking my sister places since I am grounded. Why do parents go overboard? I mean it was one class.

—Hopeless and Grounded, 14

Dear Hopeless and Grounded,

Many parents overreact when they're upset or disappointed or angry. Hopefully, she's not going to follow through on her threat to follow you around in school to be sure you go to all your classes. Your mom is probably concerned that cutting one class might be the beginning of a pattern. She wants to be sure that you understand how important attending all your classes is. Let her know that you got her message and that it won't happen again.

Dr. M

Dear Hopeless and Grounded,

Cutting class may not seem like a big deal to you, but many parents want their children to be perfect and think it's their fault if you don't follow the right path. Talk to your mom and take responsibility for what you did. It's your choice whether or not you're going to cut class again, but now you know the consequences.

Liz

What do you think?

Ask

Dr.M

and

Liz

about

Relationships

Boy Friend or Boyfriend?

Dear Dr. M and Liz,

I am really good friends with some boys. We play cards and games, and tell jokes. My problem is that some of my friends tease me about hanging out with boys. They say things like "Ooooo, Katherine has a boyfriend!" And other things that embarrass me and the boys I hang out with! What should I do?

—Katherine, 14

Dear Katherine,

You're clearly comfortable with boys and enjoy their company. While some of your friends obviously believe that any relationship with a boy has to involve romantic feelings, you are mature enough to recognize that friendships can develop with either boys or girls. Continue to choose your friends on the basis of shared fun and interests. And let the friends who tease you know that you don't appreciate the way they're acting.

Dr. M

Dear Katherine,

I can understand why you're embarrassed when your friends make those kinds of comments. I would also be embarrassed in your situation. I know that it's hard, but try not to think about them teasing you. What really matters is that you have fun with your friends, some of whom happen to be boys. Whatever you do, make sure it's what you want, not what your friends want.

Liz

Dear Dr. M and Liz,

My friends are already dating and always talking about boys. I do like boys, but I feel so left out because they think that just because I don't ask boys out, I only like girls. I am confused. Isn't there such a thing as friendship in today's world? What should I do?

— Morgan, 12

Dear Morgan,

There's no right age to start dating, but the decision should definitely be one that's made by you together with your parents. And at your age, being friends with boys without the pressure of a romantic relationship should be seen as a positive thing. You have plenty of time to start "going out" when you're older. Explain to your friends that you'll start dating when you're ready, not when they think you should.

D. M

Dear Morgan,

Although it may seem as if there can never be just friendship between a boy and a girl, you really can be friends with guys. Eventually, you may start to like one of your guy friends as more than a friend, and then you can ask him out. And if you don't, you'll still have guy friends who probably won't talk about boys all the time.

Liz

Never Been Kissed

Dear Dr. M and Liz,

I have a problem: Believe it or not, I'm 12 years old (almost 13) and I've never been kissed by a boy. All my other friends have. What's wrong with me?

—Maya, 12

Dear Maya,

First, there's absolutely nothing wrong with you! Second, at 12—almost 13—you have lots of time ahead of you to be involved in romantic relationships. Each person has her own timetable for developing physically, socially, and emotionally. You're better off waiting until you're ready than rushing into something that you're not prepared for. Consider your own needs and values rather that looking at what your friends are doing.

Dr. M

Dear Maya,

Don't worry—there's nothing wrong with you. Just because your friends have kissed boys, that doesn't mean you should, too. There is no set age when you should start kissing boys. The right time for you is whenever you feel ready, and I'm sure it doesn't matter to your friends when that is.

Liz

Too Young!

Dear Dr. M and Liz,

A boy I know asked me out and I really like him, but my mom says I can't date 'til I'm older. But I really want to go out with him. What should I do?

—Felicia, 12

Dear Felicia,

First, make sure that you, the boy, and your mom all have the same idea in mind when you're talking about dating. Your mom may be thinking about a boy and a girl going alone to a movie and out to dinner. You may be thinking of a group of friends going ice skating together. And the boy who asked you out may be thinking that a yes answer means that you like him just as he likes you, but you don't necessarily go anywhere together. I learned all this from my son when he was your age. He helped me to understand that his definition and my definition of "going out" were very different. Second, helping to set rules about dating is part of a parent's job. You may not be happy with this particular rule, but it does show that your mom is concerned about you. Try to engage your mom in a discussion about this rule and others, so both of you will have an opportunity to share your feelings and maybe arrive at some decisions both of you will feel comfortable with.

Dr. M

Dear Felicia,

I suggest that you talk to your mom about her rule. If you talk to her in a responsible way, without whining, she'll take you seriously. Then, you can explain all the reasons why you think you are old enough to date and why your mom might even like this particular boy. Since parents can often be stubborn about the rules, you may not be able to completely convince her, but you may be able to come to a compromise and at least modify the rule.

Liz

Dear Dr. M and Liz,

My boyfriend is 16 and I am 13. We've been going out for about a month and a half, but we've known each other for about three months. We have a lot in common. My parents met him about three weeks ago. My family likes him, but they don't like the idea of us.

—Confused, 13

Dear Confused,

Your boyfriend might be very nice, and it's to his credit that he's made a good impression on your parents. However, I can understand why they don't like the two of you going out. The three-year difference is very significant at your age. When you're older, the age difference will probably matter less than it does now. But a sixteen-year-old boy and a thirteen-year-old girl typically have very different expectations about dating. When my son was 16 and my daughter was 13, I didn't want my daughter choosing one of my son's friends as her boyfriend, no matter how much I liked him as my son's friend.

Dr. M

Dear Confused,

To your mom's credit, three years is a big difference and the years between 13 and 16 are important ones where you grow and mature a lot. Although you may have a lot in common with your boyfriend, there are some significant things the two of you might not understand about each other's lives. I'm not saying you two should necessarily break up, just take the age difference into consideration and maybe wait until next year, when you've started high school, to make the relationship a serious one.

Liz

Too Fast

Dear Dr. M and Liz,

I am going out with a guy who is not a prude at all. He goes way too fast with a lot of things!!! I like itsometimes, but other times it's really scary. I don't know what to do. He's nice, but I don't want to hurt his feelings. What should I do?

—Mixed Feelings, 12

Dear Mixed Feelings,

Reread your letter to me—I think you've already figured out what to do. You described "this guy's" actions as "way too fast with a lot of things," and identified your reaction some of the time as "it's really scary." You "don't want to hurt his feelings," but what about paying attention to what you're feeling? If he's as nice as you say he is, tell him how you feel and what you really want to do or not do. Honesty is critical in a relationship. Sometimes, boys behave in a certain way because they think that girls expect them to act that way. Be true to your own needs, feelings, and values. At the age of 12, you have lots of time ahead for dating. Don't rush into something you'll regret later on. Dr. M

Dear Mixed Feelings,

Since you said your boyfriend is a nice guy, just talk to him about how you feel. Next time he goes too fast, just tell him that you don't feel comfortable. If he really likes you, he'll be fine with it.

Liz

Too Risky

Dear Dr. M and Liz,

There's this boy. His name is Kyle. He says I'm his girlfriend, but we only know each other on the Internet. We don't do anything, just talk. He asked me out and I accepted. Tell me what you think.

—Debbie, 11

Dear Debbie,

The Internet can be a wonderful way to learn about new people and places, and to share ideas with others. However, there have been cases where it has been used by people who are dangerous. Kyle is probably trustworthy.

But there is a chance that he is not. He may say he's your age (11) and really be a 45-year-old man or a 17-year-old gang member. Unfortunately, since you have no sure way to know what Kyle is really like, you should NOT agree to meet him. Any time you feel uncomfortable, that's a warning sign to you. And the way you worded your note makes me think that you're uncomfortable about Kyle telling you that you're his girlfriend. Listen to your feelings.

Dr. M

Dear Debbie,

When I was your age, I had a friend who also met a boy online. They got to know each other and he told her that he wanted to meet her. I'll give you the same advice I gave her. Even though you think you know this boy and he may seem trustworthy, you don't know if he's actually who he says he is. You can still talk to him if you want to, there's no harm in that, but you shouldn't go out with him.

Liz

Taking a Chance

Dear Dr. M and Liz,

I have a major crush on a boy at school. I think he likes me, because he is constantly checking me out and looking

at me. **Every girl in my grade likes him. I don't think I have a chance, but I know he likes me and I like him. How will something ever happen if both of us don't do anything about it?**

—Dreamer, 13

Dear Dreamer,

Why do you think you don't have a chance if you know he likes you and you like him? You might think about what's preventing you from giving this boy some inkling of what you're feeling. Are you afraid you'll be rejected? That's a possibility—you could be misreading the cues. Are you afraid that the reality might not be as good as the dream? That's another possibility. Now take a look at the more positive possibilities: He'll be relieved that you took the first step, and he's even more fun in person than in your dreams. Taking a risk is often hard, but it's harder when you miss out on life because you're too afraid to take a chance.

Dr. M

Dear Dreamer,

If you think he likes you, then you do have a chance with him. But, you're right that nothing will happen if neither one of you does anything about it. You can hint that you like him by looking back at him—and smiling—when he looks at you. If he still doesn't get the hint, ask if he wants to hang out with you and see where it goes from there.

Liz

Getting Dumped

Dear Dr. M and Liz,

My boyfriend called me and told me he loved me. But the next day he dumped me!!! Does he have the problem, or do I?

—M&M, 15

Dear M&M,

Your problem was having a boyfriend who treated you in such a cruel way. His problem, which is much bigger, is being an individual who is so insensitive. Even though you probably realize that you're better off without him, it is still painful to be "dumped" in such an unexpected way. I hope your next relationship is with a guy who understands the real meaning of love—this one obviously didn't.

Dr. M

Dear M&M,

He's the one with the problem—you didn't do anything wrong. He's either confused about his feelings or he's just a jerk. If he's confused, give him some time to figure out what he wants. And in the meantime, figure out what you want. But if he's just a jerk, be glad he's out of your life.

Liz

Dear Dr. M and Liz,

If your boyfriend breaks up with you because he hears a rumor about you that's not true, what should you do?
—Ex-Girlfriend, 14

Dear Ex-Girlfriend,

Maybe you should be grateful that he's no longer your boyfriend. He broke one of the most important rules in a relationship. He didn't trust you enough to check in with you before he made the decision to break up. You may still want to set the record straight—let him know that what he heard was just not true and that he acted unfairly by jumping to a false conclusion before you had a chance to clear yourself. By the way, who started that rumor? And why? That's another piece of unfinished business you might want to take care of before a new rumor starts making the rounds.

Dear Ex-Girlfriend,

Dr. M

Tell your ex-boyfriend that what he heard is not true. If he doesn't believe you, it's time to move on. If he does believe you, your relationship might have a second chance.

Liz

What do you think?

Ask Dr. M and Liz about Feelings

Stared At

Dear Dr. M and Liz,

I am in a wheelchair and people stare at me when they're not used to me. It really bugs me. What should I do?

—Sara, 9

Dear Sara,

Your explanation is absolutely right. People stare when they're not used to seeing someone in a particular situation. You can try to educate people who stare by helping them understand that you are more than a person in a wheelchair. Being in the chair is just one aspect of who you are. You are also a nine-year-old girl with thoughts, feelings, and talents. If you feel comfortable doing so, you might ask the people who stare whether they'd like to learn more about how a wheelchair works. But the fact is, you shouldn't have to teach others how to act when they see someone who is different from themselves—accepting others is just the right thing to do.

D. M

Dear Sara,

It's natural for people to stare at people who are different in some way, even though it shouldn't be. If they haven't seen a person in a wheelchair before, they might look because they're curious. I know so many people who use wheelchairs, including my uncle and grandfather, that I would not give someone in a wheelchair a second glance. When people stare at you, you could try to ignore them. They probably just don't understand how rude they're being.

Sad and Mad

Dear Dr. M and Liz,

My grandparents are splitting up and they have been married since they were 18, and my grandma is seeing another man. My mom and I are very sad and mad at her. What should we do?

—Ria, 12

Dear Ria,

I understand why you and your mom are feeling so sad and angry, and you're probably confused, too, about why your grandparents are splitting up at this point in their lives. Try to recognize that while you can't change the situation your grandparents are in, your grandma's feelings towards you have not changed. She has left your grandfather, and not you or your mom.

Dr. M

Dear Ria,

You and your mom may not be able to change the way your grandma feels but at least you can ask her why she and your grandfather are splitting up and why she's seeing another man. Understanding the reasons more may help you to be less sad.

Liz

Not the Way It Looks

Dear Dr. M and Liz,

Everyone tells me I've got everything—the hair, the looks, and the boyfriends—but no one knows what it's really like for me. My sister is majorly ill in the hospital, my mom has breast cancer, my step-dad died a year ago, and I live with my step-mom who just divorced my dad. Everyone just thinks that nothing could go wrong in my life. PLEASE HELP ME, I BEG YOU!!!

— Hurt, 14

Dear Hurt,

Of course you are hurting with all the terrible things happening in your life. Other people may just see the outside —how you look and that you have a boyfriend. You need to let at least some of them know that you're dealing with a lot of pain right now. Trying to put on a brave front all the time adds to your stress. You probably don't want to be a burden to your family because of everything they're going through, so look for support from other adults who care about you—perhaps a counselor, a teacher, a school nurse, a relative, or a friend's parent. Allow those trusted, caring adults to be sympathetic to the sadness you're feeling.

Dr. M

Dear Hurt,

You have to learn that you don't need to put on an act for everyone. Even if you don't feel comfortable talking to all your friends about what's going on in your life, maybe there's one special, caring person you can confide in. It will be a relief to share your problems with someone.

Liz

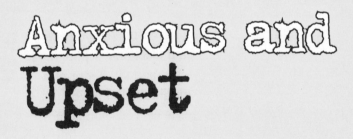

Anxious and Upset

Dear Dr. M and Liz,

Hi. I think I have a problem, but I'm not sure. I get scared over little things. Like at night, after everybody's in bed, I have to check all the doors and windows to make sure they're locked. When my mom or dad go on

a business trip, I get this weird feeling like something bad is going to happen. I even cry myself to sleep when they are gone. I've always been scared that someone will break into the house or the house will catch on fire. I get really scared sometimes. Some nights, I'll be so scared, I will just cry and cry 'til I fall asleep. Is this not right to be feeling this way? I have felt this way my whole life. What can I do?

—C.J., 13

Dear C.J.,

Have you ever told anyone—besides me—what you do and how you feel? It's important for you to share what you've told me with your mom or dad, whoever you think will listen best to you. If you feel that you can't tell your parents or if you have told them and they haven't taken you seriously, talk to a close relative, a kind teacher, a school nurse, a guidance counselor, or your doctor, and tell her or him that you have a problem and would like help in overcoming it. Everyone has some fears or is nervous sometimes, but you seem to be dealing with those feelings too much of the time. The most important part of my answer is that you can learn to be less scared and enjoy your life a whole lot more—a therapist can help you to get there.

D. M

Dear C.J.,

Everyone feels scared or nervous about those sorts of things sometimes, but if you feel like that all the time, you should sit down and talk with an adult about it. If you can let everything out that bothers you, you may find that there is some underlying issue that is causing you to have these fears. And you may realize that your fears aren't very realistic. Another thing you can do is take some time to relax to, at least temporarily, reduce your fears.

Liz

Dear Dr. M and Liz,

Sometimes my parents fight and I get upset. Sometimes I get so upset I just want to die. Can you help me?

—Steph, 10

Dear Steph,

If you haven't talked to your parents yet about how upset you get when they fight, I would suggest you do that as soon as possible. Some parents who love each other very much fight a lot. Your parents may not realize how distressing it is for you to witness their arguments. I am concerned that you wrote that sometimes you're so upset you "just want to die." Are you being dramatic to get my attention or do you truly feel that way? If the fighting is really getting to you or if you're very upset about something else, you need to talk to someone who can help you—maybe your parents or perhaps another relative or a school psychologist or counselor.

Dr. M

Dear Steph,

If you want anything to change, you're going to have to talk to your parents about how you feel, letting them know that their fighting upsets you. You may want to talk to each parent separately so they can't blame their fights on each other and then start a new one.

Liz

Dear Dr. M and Liz,

When I stay at someone else's house for the night, I always end up going home because I feel homesick at about 10 p.m. What is it, and what can I do?

—Angela, 10

Dear Angela,

While some girls might feel perfectly comfortable with a sleepover at age 8, others aren't ready until they're 11. Since you obviously want to stay overnight, you need to figure out what happens at 10 p.m. It may be that until that time, you're too busy having fun to think about your family at home. But when bedtime rolls around and the house quiets down, you begin to wonder what's happening at home or you miss the nighttime rituals with your family—perhaps a good-night hug or a quiet conversation. Before you go on your next sleepover, prepare yourself. Talk to your family about what you can do while you're at your friend's house. Maybe, you can call home just before 10 p.m. and talk to your mom or dad for a little while. You might think about what you can bring with you—something to remind you of home—perhaps a special stuffed animal or your own pillow and blanket. Also, tell yourself how proud you're going to feel when you're able to get through the night without having to go home early.

Dr. M

Dear Angela,

When I was younger I also used to get homesick at sleepovers because everyone else would fall asleep before me and I would feel so alone that I would start to miss my family and that would make it even harder to fall asleep. If you think that's why you get homesick too, at your next sleepover, you can try to imagine, or even bring with you, some comforting things that help you fall asleep at home, so you'll fall asleep before you can become homesick.

Liz

Dear Dr. M and Liz,

Lately, I've felt really gloomy. I've cried at school because I had gotten three questions wrong on my homework, and I cried at home because I couldn't remember the steps for my science test. I felt so alone, deserted— I felt like I was in a room by myself and all of a sudden the walls were coming closer and closer until every bone

in my body was being crushed. And you know what? I have lots of family, and I've got the best friend in the whole wide world. I've got everything I could ever want, so why does it seem like everything I love about myself is being eaten by this feeling? Is it because my sister died five years ago and I am in depression again, or is this just part of puberty? Please help me.

—Feeling Bad, Really Bad, 11

Dear Feeling Bad,

What you've described sounds like you are both sad and anxious. Puberty may explain some of your feelings (an increase in certain hormones during adolescence may lead to stronger emotions than you're used to), but there's more to it than that. At your age, more is expected of you in school, and that pressure may be causing you to feel stressed. Because of your sister's death, you may feel that you need to compensate—to be perfect, or close to it, to please your parents. And a recent event may have reawakened some feelings of sadness about your sister. There are many other possibilities, and you should see a counselor or therapist who can explore those possibilities with you. Today, no one has to live with the kind of emotional pain you are experiencing. You seem puzzled that you are feeling the way you do, even though you have close friends and lots of family. Please understand that you are dealing with some difficult issues, and having supportive people around is often not enough in situations such as the one you're in. Accept the support of your friends and family as you work with a therapist who can help you understand why you are feeling the way you are, and most importantly, who can help you learn effective coping techniques. *Dr. M*

Dear Feeling Bad, Really Bad,

It sounds like it's a combination of the things you mentioned—puberty plus sadness about your sister's death. Maybe something happened recently to trigger your memories of grief. Since you say you have lots of family and a very close friend, turn to them for help with dealing with your feelings. If you keep your feelings inside, no one will know that you need their help. *Liz*

Dear Dr. M and Liz,

We had a break-in one Tuesday weeks ago, and since then I've been too scared to go anywhere alone, even upstairs. What should I do about it?

—Crazy, 10

Dear Crazy,

Let me assure you that you're not crazy. But you are dealing with a stressful situation—a break-in is scary. Give yourself some time to cope with this experience. Talk to someone who can help you feel less scared—maybe a parent, a school counselor, or a doctor. Explain that you're too frightened to go anywhere alone. If your fears remain strong, you might need professional help. There's absolutely nothing wrong with getting some help when you need it. What you shouldn't do is ignore your feelings or allow your fears to take over your life.

Dr. M

Dear Crazy,

The first thing you should do is talk to the rest of your family about the break-in and how scared it has made you. They went through the same thing, so they'll understand and can help you feel better. You can also suggest to your parents that you get an alarm system or something else to protect your house against another break-in. Your family can also discuss what to do in the future if something similar happens again, so you will be more prepared and can feel safer.

Liz

Dear Dr. M,

I've started to feel afraid to go out anywhere. Every time I go out with my friends, I start to feel panicky. What is happening to me? I'm scared of going mad.

—Fool, 13

Dear "Fool,"

(I hope this advice helps you to not think of yourself in that way.) First, let me reassure you that you are not going "mad." Second, you can get help to rid yourself of these panicky feelings. What you are experiencing is anxiety. Many teens and adults feel anxious in certain situations. Counseling, therapy, and medication are all very effective ways to eliminate the sense of panic you feel. Talk (or show your letter and my response) to a school counselor or psychologist, a family physician, a parent, or another trusted adult. Don't put off telling someone because you are embarrassed. You CAN feel better!

Dr. M

Dear Fool,

Your panic attacks might be caused by something that happened in the past. If that's the case, you might be able to uncover it by talking to a parent or another adult you feel comfortable discussing personal issues with. If you can't think of anything that might have triggered these panic attacks, talk to a parent about getting help from a therapist who's specially trained to deal with these kinds of conditions. It's no fun to feel panicky all the time.

Liz

My Friend is Anorexic

Dear Dr. M and Liz,

My friend is so skinny I think she has an eating disorder. I told my school counselor, but she hasn't done anything yet. My friend was over at my house and I asked her if she wanted to have some chips and stuff like that. She always says "No!" We've been super great friends for two years now. She tells me everything so I don't think it's a point of not trusting me. I'm so worried about her. If she has an eating disorder, that means she's closer to getting sicker and sicker each day. She misses a lot of days in school. I looked up all the symptoms and all the Web pages on eating disorders. She does have some of them. I need your help! She's my best friend. I don't want her to get sicker. I've tried to talk to her, but she always stutters and changes the subject. I watch her at lunch. She doesn't eat a thing. Help!

—Worried, 12

Dear Worried,

Everyone needs a caring friend like you— someone who takes action to help a friend in trouble. You were smart to recognize that you could not deal with her problem on your own. The school counselor you spoke to may be doing something about your friend's problem. But you may not know about it because a counselor has to keep her actions confidential. She may have talked to your friend's parents or even your friend. But to be extra sure that your friend gets the help she needs—and she does need professional help if she has an eating disorder—do tell your parents or another adult you trust. Even though you are best friends, she may be embarrassed to share everything about her situation. If she does have an eating disorder, encourage her to get professional help and support her as she receives the treatment that she needs. Dr. M

Dear Worried,

You should tell your parents or your friend's parents about her problem and ask them to do something. If you tell your parents, they'll probably tell your friend's parents, and her parents will most likely get some kind of help for her. Your friend might be angry at first, but eventually she'll be glad you did something. In the long run, she'll realize you've told your parents or her parents about the situation because you wanted to help her. In the meantime, you can try to get your friend to eat or try some more to get her to talk to you about the situation she's in. Liz

My Parents
Still Smoke

Dear Dr. M and Liz,

My mom and dad smoke. I really want them to quit, and I tell them almost every day. They know it's bad and they want to quit, but they don't. Even though they don't smoke near us and they're not chain smokers, I still want them to quit. How can I get my point across to them so they'll quit?

—Amanda, 14

Dear Amanda,

You have made your point to them, and probably very well. And you and your parents have taken the first step—recognizing the problem. Unfortunately, the next steps are going to be more difficult, particularly for your mom and dad. Smoking is physically and psychologically addictive, and it's very hard for most people to quit. But many effective strategies are available—from hypnosis to patches to support groups. Your parents will need to find the one that will work for them. Your role will be to support them emotionally with encouragement and understanding as they go through the program they've selected. There is one positive in your situation—seeing firsthand how tough it is to quit smoking has probably made the habit one you'll never want to start.

Dr. M

Dear Amanda,

Show them some anti-smoking ads and statistics from websites that explain that even if they don't smoke a lot, they're more likely to get all kinds of diseases. Tell them you want them to stick around and be healthy because you love them.

Liz

What do you think?

Ask

Dr. M

and

Liz

about

Your Changing Body

Scared about Periods

Dear Dr. M and Liz,

My parents are divorced and I am worried that when I'm a bit older, I will get my period at my Dad's. I'm too afraid to ask him to buy me some pads or tampons. What should I do?

—Katie, 11

Dear Katie,

Since you won't know exactly when you will get your period for the first time, it might be a good idea to go to your dad's house prepared with a couple of sanitary pads. But keep in mind that your dad knows all about periods, so he wouldn't be surprised if you made that request. And hopefully, he'd be sensitive enough to not embarrass you.

Dr. M

Dear Katie,

If you don't want to have to ask your dad to buy you pads or tampons, the best solution is to be prepared. Ask your mom to buy pads or tampons for you and then put them in a toiletry bag that you can either take with you when you stay at your dad's house, or keep in a bathroom at his house. If you're prepared, then you won't need to ask your dad for help.

Liz

Dear Dr. M and Liz,

My mom won't talk to me about periods. I'm VERY, VERY, VERY scared that I will get it and I won't know what it is! I've heard that you get your period at age 10 and that's my age! How can I convince my mom that I NEED her to talk to me about this stuff? PLEASE GIVE ME AN ANSWER. I NEED A LOT OF HELP!!!!!!! I'M SCARED!

—Caity, 10

Dear Caity,

Some people, even moms, are embarrassed to talk about topics such as periods. And many moms have a tough time dealing with the fact that their daughters are growing up. Try telling your mom that you really need to know more about getting your period, so you'll have correct information and because not knowing is making you scared. If she still won't talk to you, find a book about growing up that can give you the information you need. Once you know the facts, you'll realize that you don't have to be scared. Getting your period is a normal part of growing up.

Dr. M

Dear Caity,

I think that if you explain to your mom that you're scared about getting your period, mainly because you don't know anything about it, she might open up to you. Talk to your mom in a mature way, showing her that you can handle whatever she has to say. It's true that some girls get their periods at age 10, but some start it as young as 8 and others as late as 16.

Liz

Am I Too Fat?

Dear Dr. M and Liz,

Sometimes I'm not happy with the way my thighs and stomach look, and I push myself over the limit and I starve myself, but I don't want to throw my period off track. I don't know what to do sometimes because I see

my aunt and she has a good body and I want one just like it. What can I do?

—Weight Problem, 10

Dear Weight Problem,

Starving yourself is not healthy no matter what your weight is! Perhaps you are not overweight, but you are striving for a body shape that is not really right for you. Try to make your goal a body that is healthy and fit, rather than one that looks exactly like your aunt's. Keep in mind that at your age, your body is changing, and has probably not reached its adult form. If you really are overweight, combine a sensible diet with a reasonable exercise regimen, which your doctor has recommended or approves of.

Dr. M

Dear Weight Problem,

Whatever you do, don't starve yourself. Besides being extremely unhealthy, it doesn't even work in the long run because you just end up eating more when you get the chance to. And not getting enough nutrients will weaken your bones and the rest of your body. If you want to look more like your aunt, ask her how she stays in shape. I'm sure she'll tell you that the best way to have a good body is not to starve yourself, but rather to eat healthier foods and be active.

Liz

Dear Dr. M and Liz,

I am overweight. I've tried EVERYTHING so people won't make fun of me. P.S. I have no friends.

—Jennifer, 10

Dear Jennifer,

While most people are caring, some can be cruel in their comments and actions. They make fun of those whom they see as too heavy, too thin, too tall, or too short. Instead of focusing on more important qualities like kindness, they make judgments based only on appearance. What is most important is how YOU feel about yourself. If being overweight bothers you, and your doctor agrees that your weight is a health problem, you can work with her/him to develop a plan to lose weight. At the same time, you can work on making friends. Lots of overweight girls have strong friendships. Ask a trusted adult—a family member, a teacher, a youth group or religious leader —to suggest ways to start a friendship. Choose one of those ideas and take action!

Dr. M

Dear Jennifer,

There are some people who just like to make fun of others. It doesn't really matter what they say about how you look. What matters is what is inside you, what kind of person you are. The kids who make fun of you aren't the ones you would want as your friends. I used to be one of the shortest girls in my class, and sometimes people teased me about that. But my real friends never did that. They like me for who I am.

Liz

Am I too Modest?

Dear Dr. M and Liz,

I am in fifth grade and I am soon to be in sixth grade. I am not nervous, except for one thing, that is gym class. I am really nervous about changing in front of other girls. It makes me uncomfortable to think this. I just want some quick tips, if you can. Please help!

—Uncomfortable, 10

Dear Uncomfortable,

Lots of girls your age feel the same way as you do. Being self-conscious is a normal and expected part of your stage of development. Everyone's body is changing at a different rate, so everyone is going to look different. Try not to compare your body to anyone else's. Focus your thoughts on your body parts that you like, and in time, you'll probably grow to be more comfortable with how you look.

D. M

Dear Uncomfortable,

When I was in the sixth grade, some of my friends changed in the bathroom stall. Others used the shower stall even though it didn't have a curtain. They just asked the others not to look. But you needed to wait five seconds because their first impulse was to look, and then they'd look away. By seventh grade, most of the girls were more comfortable changing for gym or they had figured out ways to do it while maintaining their privacy. Most people don't look anyway since they're all worried about making sure no one sees them. They won't be paying attention to you.

Liz

Do I Smell?

Dear Dr. M and Liz,

I am in Year 6, and I am developing breasts and getting pimples, but every time I ask my mum to get me some deodorant she says I don't need it, and I just feel just totally gross. I get totally embarrassed when I go to friends' houses because I am the only one who doesn't have deodorant. How can I make my mum see that I'm no longer a little kid?

—MS, 12

Dear MS,

If talking to your mother doesn't work, then perhaps writing a letter to her explaining that you're not a little kid any more will help. When you write a letter, you can keep your tone neutral, whereas when you're talking you might seem angry or whiny. Also, when you write a letter, you can organize your thoughts logically and maybe you'll be more convincing.

Dr. M

Dear MS,

If you have a book at home about puberty, you might show it to your mother, pointing out the section that states why girls your age need deodorant. If you don't have such a book, see if you can borrow one from the library or from a friend. Your mother is obviously having a tough time watching you grow up. Maybe she needs you to reassure her that although you are changing physically, you're still the daughter you've always been, just more mature.

Liz

Why Can't I Wear a Bra?

Dear Dr. M and Liz,

Most of my friends are wearing bras. My mom thinks I don't need one. How can I convince her that I'd feel better if I could wear one?

—Elizabeth, 9

Dear Elizabeth,

It's true that girls are reaching puberty (the physical changes of adolescence) earlier these days. That means that when your mom was your age, she probably remembers that girls didn't develop breasts until they were 11 or older. Now, many girls are developing at nine. It's understandable that you want to be like everyone else, so if your friends are more developed than you are and are already wearing bras, you want to wear one, too. Tell your mom that you might not need a bra yet because of your physical changes, but you do need one for social or emotional reasons. Ask her to go shopping with you, so you can show her that there are stretch bras that will fit you just fine—right now.

Dr. M

Dear Elizabeth,

To convince your mom that you'd feel better wearing a bra, you can tell her that just wanting a bra is a good reason for getting one. You should also stay calm when talking to your mom and not use the excuse "Everyone else is, why can't I?"

Liz

I'm Scared to Wear Glasses!

Dear Dr. M and Liz,

I have glasses and I am scared to wear them because I'm afraid people will make fun of me. What should I do?

—Heather, 9

Dear Heather,

Lots of kids wear glasses, and often they are a little nervous when they first start to use them. What will my friends think? Will they fall off in gym class? What will the kids in my class say? Wearing glasses will not prevent you from taking part in any of your usual activities. And there are so many pretty frames available today that some kids want to wear glasses just to look cool. Some people who may not feel very good about themselves try to build themselves up by tearing other peopl down. Remember that their mean comments say more about those individuals than about how you look in glasses. And keep thinking about how well you see now!

Dear Heather,

I wear glasses too! When I first started wearing them, I thought kids might make fun of me, but they didn't. The best part of wearing glasses is picking out new frames when my prescription changes. And they help you see better! If people make fun of you, ignore them and they'll eventually stop bothering you.

Liz

What do you think?

_____

_____

_____

_____

_____

_____

_____

_____

_____

_____

_____

_____

_____

_____

_____

What do you think? Continued

Ask Dr. M and Liz about Sisters and Brothers

My Brother Bugs Me!

Dear Dr. M and Liz,

Why do little brothers like to pick on their older sisters, and how do you make them stop?

—Frustrated, 12

Dear Frustrated,

This is a very common problem among siblings. No matter how much you and your brother love each other, you spend so much time together that you're bound to bother each other some of the time. Younger siblings are often envious of the fun and privileges older siblings seem to have. It's not easy for them to have to wait to grow up when they can see first-hand what you're involved in and allowed to do that is off-limits to them. Spend some time with him at a special time or on a special day and maybe he won't bother you the rest of the time.

Dr. M

Dear Frustrated,

It's not just little brothers who annoy their sisters, but little sisters, older brothers, and older sisters who do that, too. Siblings just behave that way, each in their own unique way. You need to make sure you don't instigate trouble, and if he starts up with you, continue to be nice to him. He might act the same way back or, at least, give up on his efforts to annoy you since they didn't work.

Liz

Dear Dr. M and Liz,

I share a bedroom with my two-year-old brother, who gets into all my things, and it seems like I have no privacy!

—Fed Up, 9

Dear Fed Up,

It's not easy sharing a room, and sharing it with a two-year-old may be the hardest situation of all. Kids of that age don't mess up things intentionally—they're just naturally curious. And they haven't yet learned the meaning of "mine and yours." You might try leaving a box of things that you don't mind giving up that your brother can play with safely. From time to time, put some new things in the box. Maybe your brother will find the contents of the box so interesting that he'll forget all about those items you don't ever want him to touch. Remember, your brother will get older, and in time he'll gain an appreciation for the ideas of ownership and privacy. But for now, keep particularly special items out of his reach.

Dr. M

Dear Fed Up,

A brother that young probably wouldn't listen to you if you tell him to stop it. But you could try. You could also talk to your mom about your problem. Possibly your mom could get you something to put your stuff in that your brother cannot open. Is there any possibility that you'd be able to get your own room?

Liz

My Sister Bugs Me

Dear Dr. M and Liz,

I usually get along with my sister, but when she is angry, I get so mad. Usually, I hold it in, but once in a while, I just burst. Do you have any suggestions on how we can stop fighting so much?

—Rebecca, 9

Dear Rebecca,

All siblings fight some of the time. That's normal. In fact, holding in your anger may make your outbursts even stronger when you finally allow your real feelings to come out.

Find a time when the two of you are getting along pretty well and talk about what makes each of you angry and what you can do when those feelings begin to threaten the peace. The hard part will be remembering what you're supposed to do when anger suddenly erupts. Keep in mind that it's OK to feel and express your anger as long as it doesn't take over a large part of your relationship.

Dear Rebecca,

Dr. M

You should talk to your parents if you haven't done that already. You can also tell your sister how you feel. Maybe you could just walk away until you're both calmer. If you don't want to "burst" with your sister, you could just close your door and scream at a pillow, even punch it if that will help.

Liz

Dear Dr. M and Liz,

My stupid sister keeps bugging the living daylights out of me. She is mentally retarded and I cannot hit her. What can I do to make her stop?!

—Mena, 17

Dear Mena,

I can tell from your letter how frustrated you are, but it's good that you recognize that hitting is not the answer. It is hard to deal with siblings under the best of circumstances—you're together so much of the time, you have to share your parents' attention, etc. But your situation is made more difficult by the fact that your sister needs more attention and probably has trouble doing some things that come so easily to you. Calling your sister "stupid" tells me how irritating her behavior is to you. Try to remember that she's doing the best that she can, and focus on what she can do rather than what she can't. It's okay to feel angry that you have to deal with a family situation that most other kids don't, but if you were to ever call her names, like "stupid," you would hurt her deeply, I want you to know that I particularly understand, since I grew up with a younger brother who has mental retardation. He sometimes tore up my school papers or pulled my hair. Although those behaviors bothered me, I never stopped loving him. And, to this day, we share an incredibly strong bond. You might also want to know that my brother is the most important reason that I became a psychologist, and I'm very grateful to him for that.

D. M

Dear Mena,

It's not your sister's fault she has mental retardation. My uncle is mentally retarded, too, and sometimes, it's hard to be around him. But I still love him. I know that you love your sister, but you can't quite understand why she acts the way she does. Maybe you could ask your mom to explain more about mental retardation, and how to better deal with your sister. You could probably give yourself and her some space when she's annoying you so you can calm down. She has feelings, and if she knows you love her, she will try to obey you when you tell her, for instance, to stop pulling your shirt. Even if she

won't listen to you, she might listen to your mom. The best
thing to do is to love your sister and try to understand.

Liz

I Lost a Brother

Dear Dr. M and Liz,

**I had one of my brothers die at less than a year old,
and I still think about him even though it is 12 years
later. But my mom and dad won't talk about him
anymore. I am afraid that they don't think about him
anymore. How can I feel better about his death,
12 years later?**

—Brother Gone, 14

Dear Brother Gone,

Even though your parents do not talk about your brother, they
have not forgotten him. Perhaps they think that you would
rather not hear about him. Let your parents know that you
would really like to be able to share your thoughts and questions with them, and that you would like them to share their
memories with you. If neither your mom nor dad are willing or

able to talk to you about your brother, share your feelings with a close friend or relative, someone who is a good listener.

D. M

Dear Brother Gone,

If your parents don't want to talk about your brother, find another relative or even a counselor at your school to talk to about your brother. You might also want to create a small memorial for your brother, using photos, poems, and pictures, anything that reminds you of him. Keep it where it's accessible, but not someplace where you have to look at it all the time.

Liz

Feeling Ditched

Dear Dr. M and Liz,

I have a big brother who is 16 years old, and he was nice to me before but now he is too cool to hang out with me. How can I get him to spend time with me? He can still have his own life and I can have mine.

—Becca, 10

Dear Becca,

The big age difference between you and your brother means that the two of you have very different interests and enjoy different activities. At 16, it's normal for him to want to spend lots of time with his friends and less time with his family. But don't think that he loves you less than he used to. Nagging him to spend more time with you will probably backfire—he'll just think of you as a pest. Maybe you could ask for his advice with a personal problem or help with homework.

Dr. M

Dear Becca,

Even if you don't understand why he doesn't want to hang out with you now, you'll probably understand his reasons in a few years. When my brother was 16, we didn't go places together, but when we were both home and didn't have other things to do, we did spend time together watching TV or talking. Try finding something fun that you'd both enjoy—it could be as simple as watching a favorite TV show together. At those moments, he'll seem like your big brother once again.

Liz

Dear Dr. M and Liz,

I have a problem with my older sister and her boy-friend. She is 16 years old and we used to be really close.

She was a really good friend to me. She is going out with her boyfriend almost one year now and I really like him. He is very nice, but the thing is I don't spend time with my sister anymore and I really miss it. I could tell her everything, but now she is with her boyfriend all the time and doesn't care about me or what I am doing. I wanted to talk with her one day about something and she said to me she doesn't have time. I don't know what to do. I really love her and I like her boyfriend too, but how should I tell her that I want to spend some time with her, too?

—Ashley, 12

Dear Ashley,

I'm sure that your sister loves you just as much as she always did, and that she's still interested in what's happening in your life. But she's just a bit preoccupied with the boy she's going out with right now. At the age of 16, that's a normal thing. Since she's the kind of person you can talk with, she'll probably come back down to earth one of these days and you'll start communicating once again. You might want to tell her how much your talks mean to you, and that you were hurt when she told you she didn't have the time to discuss something that was important to you. Make sure you let her know that you do like her boyfriend (she'll probably feel good about that) and that you know she'll be spending lots of time with him, but you want to continue the wonderful relationship you've always had with her, and that you learn a great deal from talking to her (she'll probably feel good about that, too). Be sure to speak up—she won't know how you feel until you tell her.

Dr. M

Dear Ashley,

Your sister seems very nice and considerate, but just wants time by herself and with her boyfriend. Tell your sister how you feel and ask her to spend some more time with you. Maybe you could even set some time for the two of you to be together and play games or just talk. Your sister probably doesn't realize that she isn't spending much time with you. If your sister is as nice as you say she is, then she will definitely be more considerate and will spend more time with you once she knows how you feel.

Liz

Dear Dr. M and Liz,

My brother and I used to be so close, like best buds. Now that he is older, he thinks he is too mature for me. He used to help me practice for sports, but now all he does is talk to his friends all day. I wish he could still do things with me, but I feel like he hates me. He always calls me a snot. I have a 16-year-old sister and she has her good and bad days, which are reflected in how she treats me. By the way, my brother is 15. Help!

—Help, 10

Dear Help,

Relationships change as the people in them go through different stages in their lives. Your brother still loves you very much, but he's more interested right now in being with his friends than spending time with his little sister. That's natural for a 15 year old. As you get older, the two of you will begin to establish a different kind of relationship, one in which age differences are less important and where you can talk to each other as friends and support each other as siblings. Tell your brother how you feel and how important he has always been in your life. Ask him if he can find a bit of time for the two of you to be together. And take advantage of your sister's good days to keep that relationship strong, too.

Dr. M

Dear Help,

I can understand your problem. When my brother was 15, he often ignored or annoyed me. And he would hang out with his friends a lot of the time. Sometimes, I started a conversation with him, instead of waiting for him to do that. When your brother's friends are not around, ask your brother to help you with your homework or do sports with you. Use that time to talk to him about your feelings about the relationship, and ask him how he feels about it. But don't try to compete with his friends.

Liz

My Sister Is Abusing Me

Dear Dr. M and Liz,

My 13-year-old sister abuses me and I always tell my mom that it's from softball when I fall down. She doesn't even care! I'm afraid that I might be hospitalized and my sister will continue hurting me. I don't know what to do. Please help me, I need it.

—Anna, 10

Dear Anna,

Stop making excuses for your sister, and start telling your mom the truth about your injuries. If your mom doesn't believe you, talk to another adult—someone you trust, perhaps a teacher or the school nurse. That person can help you do something about the situation you're in or can take action directly on your behalf. Your sister needs help, too, so she can learn more appropriate ways to handle her anger. You shouldn't have to be afraid in your own home.

Dr. M

Dear Anna,

When you and your mom are alone—make sure your sister is nowhere around—tell your mom what's really happening. If she doesn't know the truth, she can't help you.

Liz

My Cousin Is Mean

Dear Dr. M and Liz,

I have a cousin who is very mean and rude. He always tries to make fun of me. I try to ignore him but he keeps on picking on me and it's hard to keep ignoring him. I cannot avoid him because he lives right next to me. And at school he is one grade ahead of me, so I have to put up with him at school, too. I know that he doesn't have any friends because of his attitude, but I can't feel sorry for him anymore because of his meanness. What should I do?

— Megan, 9

Dear Megan,

You sound like a caring person — you obviously don't want to hurt your cousin's feelings. But you shouldn't have to put up with rude, mean behavior. And the fact that your cousin lives next door and goes to the same school makes the situation particularly difficult. Explain to him how his actions make other kids dislike him. He is probably trying to get attention and doesn't know that there are far better ways to reach that goal. Give him some ideas about how to be a friend. And if you ever notice even one tiny bit of nice, friendly behavior on his part, let him know that you've noticed it and that you appreciate it. Maybe there'll be more of it in the future.

Dr. M

Dear Megan,

I know how you feel because I've had experiences like that, too — with kids who are mean and rude. I think that you should talk to your cousin about his attitude. Tell him that you think he doesn't have many friends because of the way he acts. Talking to him might work or it might not, but it's worth a try.

Liz

What do you think?

_____

_____

_____

_____

_____

_____

_____

_____

_____

_____

_____

_____

_____

_____

What do you think? Continued

Ask
Dr.M
and
Liz
about
Parents

Fighting Parents

Dear Dr. M and Liz,

My parents fight a lot and my mom talks about leaving, but she never does. How can I tell her I think she should?

—Freaked over Fighting, 14

Dear Freaked over Fighting,

Relationships are very complicated. Some parents fight a lot, but they still love each other and really want to stay together. Other parents don't fight at all, but they're both miserable in the marriage. And sometimes a husband or wife will threaten to leave just to get a reaction or to encourage a spouse to change her/his behavior. Your mom needs to make her own decision about staying or leaving. But you could let her (and maybe your dad, too) know that the fighting is really getting to you. If physical violence is part of the picture and you're scared for your mom or for yourself, talk to her about that, and let her know that there are places to go for help. Talk to a school social worker or psychologist or call a local hotline to get more information about the resources—people and places—available in your community to help your family deal with this situation.

Dr. M

Dear Freaked Over Fighting,

Don't just suffer in silence. Tell your mom what you've heard and how you feel. If your mom only talks about leaving while she's fighting with your dad, it may just be a "heat of the moment" thing and she doesn't really, in her heart, want to leave. Whatever's going on between your parents, they need to know the effect those fights are having on you.

Liz

Dear Dr. M and Liz,

I have a problem. My parents yell at each other and once we had to spend the night at my grandma's house because my brothers John and Bryan and I just couldn't stand it. We burst out crying. My parents say they are going to divorce a lot, but they don't. I hope they stay together. Please help.

—Worried, 10

Dear Worried,

Some parents fight a lot and talk about divorce, but stay together because they still love each other. You need to let your parents know how much their fighting bothers you and your brothers. Or ask your grandma to tell them. If your parents decide to get divorced, it's because they can't get along with each other. Remember that they will always love you just as they do now.

Dr. M

Dear Worried,

Although you don't want your parents to get divorced, they might. It's their decision, not yours. And if they do get divorced, one advantage would be that they wouldn't be yelling at each other the way they do now. And you should know that their divorce would not be your fault or your brothers' faults either. Whatever your parents do, remember that they love you.

Liz

Dear Dr. M and Liz,

My parents fight all the time. It gets really annoying, since the fights usually happen because my brother does something or doesn't do something. I tried to explain this to my brother, but it didn't work. A couple of times the fights got so bad that my dad actually left the house and went to his office. Please, please, please help. PLEASE!

—Madison, 11

Dear Madison,

It's never easy to be around when parents fight, and it's even more frightening when a parent walks out—even if it's just temporary. While your brother may be contributing to some of the tension, your parents' arguments stem from problems that are between the two of them. It's great that you want to be the peacemaker, but your mom and dad are the ones who will have to resolve their differences. However, you might try letting them know how much their fighting bothers you.

Dr. M

Dear Madison,

Blaming your brother isn't the best way to solve your problem. Though he may be partially to blame, telling him will only make him mad, causing more fighting in your house. Your parents may be stressed from work, little problems at home make it worse, and they take it out on each other. If you and your brother cooperate with your parents and each other, your parents might not be as stressed and may not fight as much.

Liz

Absent Parents

Dear Dr. M and Liz,

My mother doesn't want to do anything with me. She does stuff with my brothers, but not with me. She tells me to leave her alone all the time. What should I do?

—Do Nothing, 9

Dear Do Nothing,

How old are your brothers? Does she spend more time with them because they're younger and need her attention? Whatever the cause, it's not fair for you to be ignored. Is there an activity you and your mom can do together that you think she'd really enjoy? Suggest it to her, and also let her know that you feel bad when she says: "Leave me alone." Sometimes, when parents feel frustrated (and the reason may have nothing to do with you), they find it difficult to think about their children's feelings. Tell your mom that you love her and want some special time for just the two of you.

Dr. M

Dear Do Nothing,

Try to talk to your mom and tell her how you feel. Then you should try to plan something fun to do together, WITHOUT your brothers. You could also talk to your brothers and ask if the next time they're doing something with your mom, they can invite you along.

Liz

Can't You Knock?

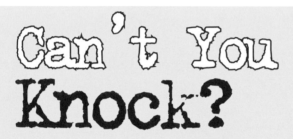

Dear Dr. M,

My parents never give me privacy. At least my dad knocks on my door now, but my mom just barges in. I locked the door once, but she got really mad and asked me why I had locked it. I want more privacy, but how can I come right out and tell her?

—Darla, 12

Dear Darla,

Since you live with your parents and see them every day, it's sometimes hard for them to recognize that you're growing up and are no longer the little girl you used to be. You have a right to expect respect for your growing privacy needs. But you have a responsibility here, too. You need to let your parents know what your needs are. And you might offer them some kind of explanation to help them feel more comfortable with how you're changing. You could try telling your mom that sometimes you need time alone to read, to try on clothes, to do your homework, to role-play a difficult situation, to play, or just to think. You could also let her know that it's embarrassing to have her barge in when your friends are over because they might make fun of the fact that you're being treated like a baby. Communicate with your mom in the most direct way you can. That way, you're more likely to get your message across.

Dr. M

Dear Darla,

Locking your door won't make your mom respect your need for privacy. If she doesn't know how you feel, she can't do anything about it. My advice is to just tell your mom how you feel. If you don't feel comfortable talking to your mom about this, tell your dad since he seems to respect your need for privacy. He can talk to your mom without having you feel embarrassed. This is what I did when I had this problem—except it was my dad who had a hard time dealing with my need for privacy and my mom who understood and helped my dad see my point of view.

Liz

Too Much Responsibility

Dear Dr. M and Liz,

I have five brothers and one sister. Whenever I have plans with my friends, my parents always ask me to baby-sit right as I'm walking out the door. What can I do?

—Too Many Sisters and Brothers, 12

Dear Too Many Sisters and Brothers,

Let your parents know that you would like to help out with your brothers and sister, but you'd appreciate being consulted in advance so you can be sure you'll be free to take care of them. Explain that it's hard for you to change plans at the last minute, and that it's not really fair to your friends to do so. Maybe you and your parents can work out a weekly schedule, so everyone will know what's expected. Of course, if your parents need you to baby-sit in an emergency, I know they'd be grateful for your help.

Dr. M

Dear Too Many Sisters and Brothers,

Before you make plans with your friends, ask your parents whether they'll need you to baby-sit. That way, if you're walking out the door and they ask you to baby-sit, remind them that you had already asked if you would be needed, and since they said no, you made other plans. Hopefully, they'll allow you to go out with your friends, and they'll give you more notice in the future.

Liz

But MOM!

Dear Dr. M and Liz,

I am really into gymnastics and I'm really good, too. Recently, I was invited to join a gymnastics team, which has been my goal for a long time. I was very excited, but my mom said I couldn't join the team. I think that it is extremely unfair. What should I do?

—Gym Bum, 9

Dear Gym Bum,

I can understand how disappointed you must be. Ask your mom why she doesn't want you to join the team. She may have a good reason or maybe she just doesn't realize how important gymnastics is in your life. I do know that parents generally make decisions because they believe their actions are in the best interests of their children. Sometimes those decisions are appropriate, but at other times, the decisions are made without considering all the facts (including the opinions of their kids).

Dr. M

Dear Gym Bum,

With your mom, list pros and cons of joining the team. And maybe if she realizes that there are more pros than cons, she'll change her mind. I used to take gymnastic classes and really enjoyed them. Now dance is my thing.

Liz

Dear Dr. M and Liz,

My mom really wants me to play piano. I play both piano and flute, but I REALLY, REALLY want to play flute. One time my mom dragged me to the piano and made me play. What should I do?

—Flutist (not Pianist), 13

Dear Flutist (not Pianist),

Ask your mom why she insists on having you play the piano when you don't enjoy it. Maybe she regrets the fact that she didn't take lessons when she was younger and she doesn't want you to lose out on that opportunity. Perhaps she bought a piano because you had expressed an interest in that instrument, and now it's just collecting dust most of the time. Whatever her reason, making you play is not fair to you. You're at an age when you have strong interests, and clearly piano playing is not one of them. And the more she forces you to play, the less likely it is that you'll ever really enjoy playing. If your mom won't listen, talk to another adult in your life who might be able to help your mom see your side of the story.

Dr. M

Dear Flutist (not Pianist),

Try to explain to your mom that you would much rather play the flute than the piano, and give her your reasons. If she doesn't understand your reasons, try to explain them in another way. Tell her that you like music and don't mind practicing, but piano is not right for you. Keep practicing the piano when your mom insists on it, but show your mom how much more you like the flute by practicing that instrument every chance you get.

Liz

Dear Dr. M and Liz,

My mom always asks questions and tries to figure out why I'm not always ecstatic when I come home from

school. She doesn't understand that sometimes I have bad days at school and don't want to talk about it or just plain don't want to deal with the questions. When I try to tell her about this, she just gets upset. How should I tell her to stop asking so many questions and commenting when I'm not always happy.

—Cocoa Butter, 9

Dear Cocoa Butter,

When you come home from school, you probably need some time to unwind from your long day. And if you've had a particularly bad day, the last thing you need is your mom throwing questions at you about situations you probably want to forget about, at least for a while. That's what you need to talk to your mom about. When you just tell her to stop asking questions, she probably gets even more concerned about your state of mind. Let her know that you appreciate her concerns, and that you'll talk to her when you're ready. Reassure her that kids your age are not always happy and that that's perfectly normal. Tell her that if there's something to worry about, you'll let her know right away. Also let her know that you'd rather not discuss some situations. Remember that your mom loves you, and that it's hard for her to see you unhappy.

Dr. M

Dear Cocoa Butter,

Maybe your mom won't get upset if you tell her in a nice, calm way that sometimes you have bad days. And that it's not a big deal. If you talk to your mom in an angry way, she'll probably respond in the same way. I understand how you feel—sometimes my mom asks me questions that I don't want to answer. I have to remind her that when she has bad days, she doesn't always want to talk to the rest of us right away.

Dear Dr. M and Liz,

Liz

I throw tantrums about doing chores. My parents and sister always yell at me to put my dishes away or pick up my stuff. I HATE CLEANING! I would rather play video games or even practice my instrument—anything to keep me from doing my chores. Is there anything I can do to stop my problem?

—Too Many Chores, 12

Dear Too Many Chores,

I'm not too fond of doing chores either, but they have tget done if we want to have a clean house, meals to eat, and clothes that look presentable. In our family, we've tried all kinds of strategies to make doing chores fairer and less unpleasant for all of us. But the fact is, everyone would rather be doing something else, including your mom and sister. So, with your family brainstorm some ideas that will help you to get the work done. One of our techniques is to have a one- or two-hour period every weekend when we all work together to do the chores that most need to get done. We often put music on or talk while we work, and the time seems to go by relatively quickly.

Dr. M

Dear Too Many Chores,

I used to have the same problem, but now my chores are more fun because we usually work together. One solution that worked in my family was to trade chores. My brother gave me one of his chores that I didn't really mind doing, and I gave him one of mine that I hated but he was willing to do. Also think of doing chores as a habit. After a while, you get used to doing them.

Liz

Why Can't You Keep a Secret?

Dear Dr. M and Liz,

Sometimes it's a lot easier talking to my friends than to my mom. When I tell my mom something that I don't want anybody to know, she'll tell everybody!!! What do I do?

—Alexis, 10

Dear Alexis,

Growing up is not easy for either daughters or moms, and both of you are figuring out how to deal with your changing relationship. Remember that she's learning along with you. Before you share something confidential with your mom, remind her to keep what you say private. Let her know that much as you want to talk to her about certain topics, you can't do that if she tells others what you have revealed to her. Even if your mom keeps all of what you say confidential, you might still want to talk about certain issues with your friends, and that's a part of growing up, too.

D. M

Dear Alexis,

Tell your mom that you don't like it when she tells others about your personal stuff, and that's the reason you don't talk to her very much. Your mom may not realize that what you're telling her is supposed to stay between the two of you. Make it clear when something is private. It's normal for you to talk with your friends about certain topics, but make sure you don't block your mom out of your life. She may have good advice. And the facts that she gives you are more likely to be true than any of the rumors that you hear from your friends.

Liz

What do you think?

_____

_____

_____

_____

_____

_____

_____

_____

_____

_____

_____

_____

_____

_____

Doodles

Doodles Cont.

About Girl Scouts your way...

With nearly 3 million girl members, there is plenty of room for you!

Girls have a lot to say—as do your families, your peers, the media, and your communities. In a time when pressures bombard girls from every side, you say you want a place where others listen to you, a place where your voices are heard.

Girl Scouts responds to you by providing a supportive environment in which you can find friends, gain new knowledge and understanding about the world and yourselves, and have some serious fun.

Preteen and teen girls helped to create a "By Girls, for Girls" approach to Girl Scouting. It's Girl Scouts your way and includes all of the things you love to do —traveling to exotic locations, learning about college and careers, developing leadership skills, improving the community, or just hanging out with other girls where there's no pressure. And caring adult advisers are available when you need someone to talk to, or to help you make plans.

For more information about how you can get involved in Girl Scouts, visit us online at:

www.studio2b.org
www.gogirlsonly.org
www.girlsgotech.org
www.girlscouts.org